COOKING
for
CHRISTMAS

A Cook's Countdown to Planning the Perfect Christmas

Linda Doeser

Bath · New York · Singapore · Hong Kong · Cologne · Delhi · Melbourne

This edition published by Parragon in 2008

Parragon
Queen Street House
4 Queen Street
Bath BA1 1HE, UK

Produced by The Bridgewater Book Company Ltd

Photographers: Ian Parsons & David Jordan
Home Economists: Richard Green, Brian Wilson & Jacqueline Bellefontaine

ISBN 978-1-4075-4354-3

Printed in China

NOTES FOR THE READER

- This book uses imperial, metric, or US cup measurements. Follow the same units of measurement throughout; do not mix imperial and metric.

- All spoon measurements are level: teaspoons are assumed to be 5 ml, and tablespoons are assumed to be 15 ml.

- Unless otherwise stated, milk is assumed to be whole, eggs and individual vegetables such as carrots are medium, and pepper is freshly ground black pepper.

- Recipes using raw eggs should be avoided by infants, the elderly, pregnant women, convalescents, and anyone suffering from an illness.

Contents

INTRODUCTION

Fine food and edible treats are among the most traditional and best-loved aspects of Christmas, especially if you are sharing them with family and friends. For the family cook, however, the whole event can be quite stressful and involve a lot of hard work. This book is designed to make all the preparation and cooking as trouble-free as possible, so that everyone has a really enjoyable time. It is divided into four chapters, to make planning your Christmas entertaining easy.

Even if you usually leave your Christmas shopping until just before Christmas Eve, you will find the recipes in the first chapter, The Festive Season, invaluable for getting a head start on your Christmas catering. You may even decide to make some edible gifts. The recipes allocated to Christmas Eve include many special touches that we often intend to add but never quite get round to. Preparing them on Christmas Eve ensures that they are not overlooked. The third chapter, Christmas Day, is packed with all the traditional favorites to make your Christmas meal a sparkling and memorable occasion, including a fabulous breakfast to help you start the day in style. The last chapter, The Day After Christmas, offers some ingenious ways with leftovers and some tempting dishes to counterbalance the richness of the Christmas feast, while still maintaining a mood of celebration.

Timing the preparations for the main Christmas meal and the other festive meals can be complicated, so a timetable for each chapter is included in the following pages. These will help you avoid such common hiccups as finding that the potatoes are still rock hard when everything else is ready to be served or suddenly realizing at midnight on Christmas Eve that you

GUIDE TO RECIPE KEY

Simplicity

Recipes are graded as easy, very easy, or extremely easy.

Preparation time

Where marinating, chilling, or cooling are involved, these times have been added on separately: e.g. 15 minutes + 30 minutes to marinate.

Cooking time

Cooking times do not include the cooking of side dishes or accompaniments served with the main dishes.

Number of servings

Recipes generally serve six to eight people. Simply divide proportionately when catering for fewer people.

have forgotten to frost the cake. These timetables won't take the work out of Christmas cooking, but they will make it very much easier to organize. Simply refer to the dishes that you plan to cook yourself for Christmas.

All the eagerly anticipated seasonal delights are here, from Roast Turkey with Bread Sauce to Mulled Wine, Plum Pudding, and Irish Coffee. There are some delicious nibbles and cocktails to serve before the meal, tasty appetizers, a choice of dressings to accompany the turkey or goose, even a delicious roast for any vegetarians in the family. As well as familiar favorites such as Apple Pies, there are also some more unusual Christmas specialities such as Sloe Gin.

Take time to browse through the pages before you decide what you want to serve over Christmas this year. Be selective; if you are going to make Orange Rum Hard Sauce, you don't need to make Hard Sauce as well. If you're not keen on the traditional Christmas fruitcake, opt for the ever-popular chocolate Bûche de Noël instead.

Enlist the help of the family—everyone can manage to do something, even if it's just rolling Chocolate Truffles in unsweetened cocoa. Get the children to hand out the nibbles and make people take turns in the kitchen cleaning up.

Whether you are planning a massive family gathering or just a quiet Christmas for two, you are sure to find the perfect dish, the ideal drink, and a self-indulgent treat that will make the day extra special.

TIMETABLES

Festive Season

Getting part of the main Christmas cooking completed well in advance makes everything so much easier when the great day comes. Some foods actually benefit from being made ahead of time.

COUNTDOWN

SEPTEMBER–OCTOBER
Bottle Sloe Gin (see page 29) to give it time to mature for Christmas.

NOVEMBER
Make the Christmas Cake (see page 17). Fruitcake keeps well and can be made even more delicious by occasionally "feeding" it with brandy.

Make the Plum Pudding (see page 14). The traditional date for doing this is the last Sunday before Advent. Follow the custom of letting everyone in the family stir and wish three times.

Check stocks in the drinks cabinet and replenish supplies if necessary.

DECEMBER
Cookies, snacks, and sponge cakes for Christmas Day itself cannot be made very far in advance, although unfilled Brandy Snaps (see page 22) can be stored in an airtight container. The dough for Cheese Straws (see page 30) can also be made in advance and stored in the freezer. Thaw at room temperature before rolling out and baking. Such homemade festive nibbles make a welcome treat for pre-Christmas visitors.

Remember to allow at least 24 hours after covering the Christmas cake with marzipan before frosting it. The frosting also needs time to set.

Make a list of all the ingredients you will require and plan your shopping carefully. Place any special orders early in the month, but don't buy fresh vegetables or fruit too far in advance. Check the use-by dates on pantry items, such as flour, to avoid any last-minute panics.

TIMETABLES

Christmas Eve

For some, Christmas Eve provides an opportunity to get some early preparation done for Christmas Day, while others like to start the celebrations.

COUNTDOWN

MORNING

Check that you have bought all the ingredients you will need for the next few days, because this may be your last opportunity before the celebrations begin.

If you prepare Poached Salmon (see page 39) early, it is an ideal recipe to serve cold either on Christmas Eve or Christmas Day.

This is a good time to get a head start on all those special little extras—Cranberry Sauce (see page 36), Orange Rum Hard Sauce (see page 42), Hard Sauce (see page 44), and Stuffed Dates (see page 50).

To be sure of well-chilled drinks over the festivities, make extra supplies of ice cubes during the day and store them in a plastic bag in the freezer.

AFTERNOON

Make Chicken Liver Pâté (see page 34) if it is on the Christmas Day or Christmas Eve menu. Make Melba toast (thinly sliced bread toasted until brown and crisp) at the same time and store it in an airtight container.

You may need to bake more than one batch of Apple Pies (see page 40), as they are so tempting when still warm.

EVENING

Hot Rum Punch (see page 47) and Mulled Ale or Wine (see page 48), provide a warm welcome for visitors. Even if you're not entertaining, a glass will put you in a festive mood while you're making last-minute preparations.

Lay the table for the Christmas meal to save time in the morning and try to leave the kitchen as tidy as possible.

Christmas Day

This requires almost military precision. The following countdown is for a 2.00 pm meal, but you can easily adjust the timing if you want to serve the meal earlier or later. The cooking time will also need to be increased if your turkey and ham are larger than those stipulated.

COUNTDOWN

BREAKFAST
Scrambled Eggs with Smoked Salmon (see page 54) is quick, easy, and special.

9.00–9.30 am Make Chestnut and Sausage Dressing (see page 59) or Mushroom Dressing (see page 60). Put white wine and champagne in refrigerator.

9.15 am Start the Glazed Ham (see page 66).

9.45 am Preheat the oven, and prepare and stuff the Roast Turkey (see page 62).

10.00 am Put the turkey in the oven. Preheat the oven and stuff the Roast Goose (see page 65) before cooking.

11.00 am Prepare the Vegetarian Roast (see page 69) to allow time for cooling. Start steaming the Plum Pudding.

11.15 am Preheat the oven for the Vegetarian Roast.

11.30 am Put the Vegetarian Roast in the oven.

12.00 noon Start making the Bread Sauce (see page 62) to allow time for the milk to infuse.

12.30 pm Prepare and start cooking Perfect Roast Potatoes (see page 70). Remove the Cranberry Sauce from the refrigerator to bring to room temperature.

12.30–1.00 pm Make and serve Champagne Cocktails (see page 56). Open red wine to allow time for it to breathe.

12.45 pm Prepare the Brussels Sprouts with Chestnuts (see page 73).

1.00 pm Prepare the Glazed Parsnips (see page 74). Make the Festive Shrimp Cocktail (see page 76).

1.30 pm Remove the roast from the oven, cover loosely with foil, and let rest for about 15 minutes before carving or slicing.

2.00 pm Begin to serve the appetizer.

Relax and make Irish Coffee (see page 78) before the big clean-up begins.

The Day After Christmas

This is traditionally a day for relaxing and you won't want to follow a strict timetable if you have been entertaining the day before. However, you may find it helpful to have a countdown for a 1.00 pm lunch.

COUNTDOWN

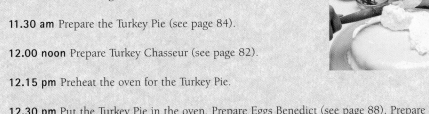

10.00 am Make Tipsy Cake (see page 93) to allow time for cooling and chilling. Make Fruit Compote (see page 94) to allow time for chilling.

11.30 am Prepare the Turkey Pie (see page 84).

12.00 noon Prepare Turkey Chasseur (see page 82).

12.15 pm Preheat the oven for the Turkey Pie.

12.30 pm Put the Turkey Pie in the oven. Prepare Eggs Benedict (see page 88). Prepare Turkey Curry (see page 87). Prepare Coleslaw (see page 90) and/or Waldorf Salad (see page 90), and wash any salad greens and vegetables.

THE FESTIVE SEASON: PERFECT PREPARATIONS

There is always a lot to do over Christmas so it is worth doing some careful planning well in advance. Make a list of the food that you intend to serve, but don't be too ambitious or you'll end up exhausted and won't enjoy yourself. The recipes in this chapter can be cooked in advance, taking some of the stress out of festive entertaining.

Both Plum Pudding (see page 14) and Christmas Cake (see page 17) can be made in November or even earlier, as they taste better if given time to mature. In any case, you will need to allow time for decorating the cake so the baking really shouldn't be left to the last minute. Some of the other Christmas goodies, such as the traditional Bûche de Noël (see page 18), must be made closer to the day—perhaps in the week leading up to Christmas.

Busy mothers will be well aware that this is also the season for parties and Christmas fairs at school. Some of the recipes in this chapter, such as Gingerbread Figures (see page 21) and Frosted Stars (see page 24), are perfect for such events because they are quick and easy to make.

𝒫lum pudding

 very easy   45 minutes   9 hours (6 hrs plus 3 hrs)   serves 8

INGREDIENTS

butter, for greasing
generous 3/4 cup self-rising flour
1/2 tsp freshly grated nutmeg
1/2 tsp ground cloves
1/2 tsp ground cinnamon
1/2 tsp salt
1 1/2 cups shredded suet
3 cups fresh white bread crumbs
2 cups raisins
1 1/3 cups golden raisins
generous 1 1/2 cups currants
1/4 cup slivered almonds
generous 1/8 cup candied cherries, chopped
1/3 cup chopped candied peel
1 cooking apple, peeled, cored, and grated
finely grated rind and juice of 1/2 orange
finely grated rind and juice of 1/2 lemon
5 tbsp stout or beer
3 eggs, lightly beaten

TO SERVE
1/4 cup brandy
Orange Rum Hard Sauce (see page 42) or Hard Sauce (see page 44)
heavy cream

Grease a 7-cup ovenproof bowl. Cut out a large circle of waxed paper and a large circle of foil. Lay the two sheets together, grease the waxed paper and, holding them together, fold a pleat in the center of the circles to allow room for the pudding to rise during steaming.

Sift the flour, spices, and salt together into a large bowl and stir in the  suet, bread crumbs, dried fruit, almonds, cherries, candied peel, apple, orange, and lemon rind. Mix together the stout or beer, orange and lemon juice, and eggs, then stir into the dry ingredients. Mix thoroughly, then spoon into the bowl. Cover with the pleated circles, waxed-side down, and tie securely with string. Place the bowl in a pan; pour in enough boiling water to come halfway up the side of the bowl, and steam the pudding for 6 hours, adding more boiling water as necessary. Do not allow the pan to boil dry.

Let cool, then remove the cover and replace with fresh waxed and foil circles. Store the pudding in its bowl in a cool place until required.

To serve, steam the pudding for an additional 3 hours. Uncover the top and run a knife blade around the inside of the bowl, then turn out onto a warm dish. Gently heat the brandy in a ladle, then pour over the pudding and ignite. Serve with the orange rum hard sauce or hard sauce and cream.

Christmas cake

 easy

 30 minutes, plus frosting, decorating, and drying

 about 3¹/₂ hours

 makes 1 x 8-inch/20-cm cake

INGREDIENTS

8 oz/225 g unsalted butter, plus extra for greasing
scant 1 cup (packed) brown sugar
4 eggs
scant 1⁵/₈ cups all-purpose flour
1 tsp allspice
¹/₂ tsp ground cinnamon
pinch of freshly grated nutmeg
pinch of salt
2 tbsp brandy, plus extra for feeding
grated rind of 1 lemon
1¹/₃ cups golden raisins
generous 1¹/₂ cups currants
scant 1¹/₂ cups raisins
²/₃ cup chopped candied peel
¹/₃ cup candied cherries, coarsely chopped
generous ³/₈ cup blanched almonds, finely chopped

TO DECORATE

generous ¹/₂ cup apricot jelly
1¹/₄ lb/550 g marzipan
3 egg whites
1 lb 9 oz/700 g confectioners' sugar, sifted
1 tbsp lemon juice
Christmas figures, holly leaves, edible silver balls, ribbon, cake frill, etc.

Grease and line an 8-inch/20-cm round cake pan. Preheat the oven to 300°F/150°C.

Cream the butter and sugar together until light and fluffy. Beat in the eggs, one at a time, alternating with 1 tablespoon flour. Sift the remaining flour, spices, and salt together into the bowl and fold in. Gently mix in the brandy. Mix together the lemon rind, dried fruit, peel, cherries, and almonds and fold in. Spoon the batter into the prepared pan and level the surface. Wrap several layers of newspaper around the outside of the pan and bake the cake for about 3¹/₂ hours, until a skewer inserted into the center comes out clean.

Place the cake, still in the pan, on a wire rack to cool, then turn out. If you like, before storing, pierce the cake several times on the base with a toothpick, and pour 2–3 tablespoons brandy over it. Store, wrapped up in a cool place.

To decorate, heat the jelly with 2–3 tablespoons water, stirring occasionally, until melted. Pass through a strainer into a clean pan and bring to a boil. Let simmer until the mixture reaches a coating consistency. Let cool, then brush the top and side of the cake with the glaze. Roll out the marzipan and use to cover the top and side of the cake smoothly. Store, uncovered, for at least 24 hours before frosting.

To frost the cake, beat the egg whites until frothy, then gradually beat in half the confectioners' sugar with a wooden spoon. Beat in the lemon juice and half the remaining sugar. Gradually beat in enough of the remaining sugar to form soft peaks. Cover and let stand to allow air bubbles to escape, then coat the cake with the frosting using a spatula. Raise into small peaks and decorate to taste. Let set in a cool place.

Bûche de Noël

 easy   35 minutes, plus frosting and decorating   15 minutes   serves 8

INGREDIENTS

butter, for greasing

generous ³/₄ cup all-purpose flour, plus extra for dusting

scant ³/₄ cup superfine sugar, plus extra for sprinkling

4 eggs, separated

1 tsp almond extract

10 oz/280 g semisweet chocolate, broken into squares

1 cup heavy cream

2 tbsp rum

confectioners' sugar, for dusting

Preheat the oven to 375°F/190°C. Grease and line a 16 x 11-inch/40 x 28-cm jelly roll pan and dust with flour.

Set aside 2 tablespoons of the sugar and whisk the remainder with the egg yolks until thick and pale. Stir in the almond extract. Whisk the egg white in a clean, greasefree bowl until soft peaks form. Gradually whisk in the reserved sugar until stiff and glossy. Sift half the flour over the egg yolk mixture and fold in, then fold in one-quarter of the egg whites. Sift and fold in the remaining flour, followed by the remaining egg whites. Spoon the batter into the pan, spreading it out evenly with a spatula. Bake for about 15 minutes, until light golden.

Sprinkle superfine sugar over a sheet of waxed paper and turn out the cake onto the paper. Roll up and let cool.

Place the chocolate in a heatproof bowl. Bring the cream to boiling point in a small pan, then pour over the chocolate and stir until it has melted. Beat with an electric mixer until smooth and thick. Set aside about one-third of the chocolate mixture and stir the rum into the remainder.

Unroll the cake and spread the chocolate and rum mixture over it. Reroll and cut off a small piece diagonally at one end and arrange a piece on the side to represent a branch. Place the cake on a plate. Spread the reserved chocolate mixture evenly over the top and sides. Draw the tines of a fork along the coating to resemble bark. Store in a cool place or the refrigerator until required. Just before serving, decorate with a sprig of holly and sift a little confectioners' sugar over the log to represent snow.

Gingerbread figures

 very easy 30 minutes, plus 30 minutes chilling, cooling, and setting 12 minutes makes 12

INGREDIENTS

generous ³/₄ cup all-purpose flour, plus extra for dusting

¹/₂ tsp ground ginger

¹/₂ tsp ground cinnamon

¹/₂ tsp baking soda

2 tbsp unsalted butter, plus extra for greasing

2 tbsp corn syrup

generous ¹/₄ cup (packed) brown sugar

1–2 tsp milk (if necessary)

GLACÉ FROSTING

¹/₂ cup confectioners' sugar, sifted

1–2 tsp lukewarm water

few drops of food coloring (optional)

edible colored balls

Sift the flour, ginger, cinnamon, and baking soda together into a bowl. Heat the butter, syrup, and sugar in a small pan over low heat, stirring occasionally, until melted and combined. Remove from the heat and let cool slightly, then add to the flour mixture and mix to a firm dough, adding milk if necessary. Form into a ball, wrap in plastic wrap, and let chill for 30 minutes.

Preheat the oven to 325°F/160°C. Grease 2 baking sheets. Roll out the dough on a lightly floured counter to ¹/₄ inch/5 mm thick and stamp out figures with a gingerbread cutter. Place the figures on the baking sheets and bake for about 12 minutes, until just firm. Using a spatula, carefully transfer to wire racks to cool.

To make the glacé frosting, sift the sugar into a bowl and gradually stir in enough water to give a consistency that will coat the back of the spoon. Add a few drops of food coloring if you choose. Spoon the frosting into a pastry bag fitted with a fine, plain tip. Pipe eyes, noses, and mouths and decorate the figures with buttons and edgings. Let set, then store in an airtight container. Press some colored balls into the frosting for eyes, nose, and buttons.

Brandy snaps

 very easy 15 minutes, plus cooling and setting 2½ hours Makes 36

INGREDIENTS

oil, for oiling
4 oz/115 g unsalted butter
²/₃ cup corn syrup
generous ½ cup raw brown sugar
generous ¾ cup all-purpose flour
2 tsp ground ginger
2½ cups stiffly whipped heavy cream, to serve

Preheat the oven to 325°F/160°C. Brush a nonstick baking sheet with oil. Place the butter, syrup, and sugar in a pan and set over low heat, stirring occasionally, until melted and combined. Remove the pan from the heat and let cool slightly. Sift the flour and ground ginger together into the butter mixture and beat until smooth. Spoon 2 teaspoons of the batter onto the baking sheet, spacing them well apart. Bake for 8 minutes, until pale golden brown. Keep the remaining batter warm. Meanwhile, oil the handle of a wooden spoon. Remove the baking sheet from the oven and let stand for 1 minute so the brandy snaps

firm up slightly. Remove one with a spatula and immediately curl it around the handle of the wooden spoon. Once set, carefully slide off the handle, and transfer to a wire rack to cool completely. Repeat with the other brandy snap. On a cool baking sheet, bake the remaining batter and shape in the same way. Do not be tempted to cook more than 2 brandy snaps at a time or the circles will set before you have time to shape them. When all the brandy snaps are cool, store in an airtight container.

To serve, spoon the heavy cream into a pastry bag fitted with a star tip. Fill the brandy snaps with cream from both ends.

Frosted stars

extremely easy   30 minutes plus chilling, cooling, and setting   8–10 minutes   Makes 30–36

INGREDIENTS

6 oz/175 g unsalted butter
1¹/₂ cups vanilla sugar
1 egg, plus 1 egg yolk
grated rind of ¹/₂ orange
generous 2 cups all-purpose flour, plus extra for dusting
pinch of salt
4 x quantity Glacé Frosting (see page 21)
edible silver balls

Cream together the butter and vanilla sugar until light and fluffy. Gradually mix in the egg, egg yolk, and orange rind. Sift the flour and salt together over the mixture and fold in to make a dough. Gather the dough into a ball, wrap in plastic wrap, and let chill for 30 minutes.

Preheat the oven to 375°F/190°C. Roll out the dough on a lightly floured counter to ¹/₈–¹/₄ inch/3–5 mm thick. Stamp out shapes with a lightly floured star cutter and place on 2 nonstick baking sheets. Gather up and reroll the trimmings to make more stars. Bake for 8–10 minutes, until light golden brown. Transfer to a wire rack to cool completely.

When cold, spread the glacé frosting over the stars, and arrange the silver balls in a decorative pattern on top. Let set, then store in an airtight container.

Chocolate truffles

  extremely easy   15 minutes, plus setting   5 minutes Makes 18

INGREDIENTS

4¹/₂ oz/125 g semisweet chocolate, broken into pieces

2 tbsp brandy, rum, or whiskey

3 tbsp unsalted butter, diced

¹/₂ cup confectioners' sugar, sifted

generous ¹/₂ cup ground almonds

unsweetened cocoa, for dusting

Place the chocolate in a heatproof bowl and melt over a pan of barely simmering water. Do not allow the base of the bowl to touch the surface of the water. Remove from the heat, stir in the brandy, rum, or whiskey, and let cool slightly. Beat in the butter, sugar, and almonds until thoroughly combined. Shape the mixture into 18 small balls and place on a sheet of parchment paper.

Sift the unsweetened cocoa into a shallow dish or onto a plate. Roll each of the balls in the cocoa to coat, shake off the excess, and leave on the parchment paper until set. Store in an airtight container, interleaving the layers with parchment paper.

Sloe gin

 extremely easy
 25 minutes, plus 3 months standing
 none
 makes about 3 cups

INGREDIENTS

12 oz/350 g sloes
scant 1 cup superfine sugar
3¹/₂ cups gin

Rinse the sloes thoroughly and remove the stalks. Prick them all over with a toothpick. Pack the sloes into a sterilized preserving jar, sprinkling each layer with sugar. Pour in the gin and seal the jar. Store in a cool, dark place for 3 months, shaking the jar occasionally.

Strain the gin into a pitcher, then pour into a sterilized bottle, seal, and label. The sloe gin will be ready for drinking, but may be stored for up to 1 year—next Christmas, in fact.

Cheese straws

 very easy   30 minutes 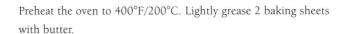 10 minutes   serves 10–12

INGREDIENTS

4 oz/115 g unsalted butter, plus extra for greasing

generous ³/₄ cup all-purpose flour, plus extra for dusting

pinch of salt

pinch of paprika

1 tsp mustard powder

³/₄ cup grated cheese, such as Cheddar or Gruyère

1 egg, lightly beaten

1–2 tbsp cold water

poppy seeds, for sprinkling

Preheat the oven to 400°F/200°C. Lightly grease 2 baking sheets with butter.

Sift the flour, salt, paprika, and mustard powder into a bowl. Add the butter, cut it into the flour with a knife, then rub in with your fingertips until the mixture resembles bread crumbs. Stir in the cheese and add about half the beaten egg. Then mix in enough water to make a firm dough. The dough may be stored in the freezer. Thaw at room temperature before rolling out.

Spread out the poppy seeds on a shallow plate. Turn the dough onto a lightly floured counter and knead briefly, then roll out. Using a sharp knife, cut the dough into strips measuring about 4 x ¹/₄ inch/ 10 x 0.5 cm. Brush with the remaining beaten egg and roll some or all of the straws in the poppy seeds to coat, then arrange them on the baking sheets. Gather up the dough trimmings and reroll. Stamp out 10–12 circles with a 2¹/₂-inch/6-cm fluted cutter, then stamp out the centers with a 2-inch/5-cm plain cutter. Brush with beaten egg and place on the baking sheets.

Bake for about 10 minutes, until golden brown. Leave the cheese straws on the baking sheets to cool slightly, then transfer to wire racks to cool completely. Store in an airtight container. Thread the pastry straws through the pastry rings before serving.

CHRISTMAS EVE: THE FINAL COUNTDOWN

Christmas morning is bound to be a busy time for the family cook so anything that can be done the day before will save valuable time. The recipes in this chapter include many extras that make all the difference to the Christmas meal but there is seldom enough time to make them on the day. Homemade Cranberry Sauce (see page 36) and Hard Sauce (see page 44), for example, are much tastier than their ready-made counterparts and are quick and easy to make in advance and store overnight in the refrigerator.

Chicken Liver Pâté (see page 34) is always a popular appetizer and this, too, can be made the day before. Poached Salmon (see page 39) is ideal for a Christmas evening buffet as it looks wonderful and is a pleasant contrast to the roast turkey or goose eaten earlier in the day. Prepare it on Christmas Eve to avoid having to spend any extra time in the kitchen on Christmas Day. Gluttons for punishment who intend to entertain on Christmas Eve as well as Christmas Day will also find both these recipes ideal for a festive Christmas Eve menu. For a more informal gathering, you might offer Hot Rum Punch (see page 47) and warm Apple Pies (see page 40).

Chicken liver pâté

INGREDIENTS

7 oz/200 g butter

8 oz/225 g trimmed chicken livers, thawed if frozen

2 tbsp Marsala or brandy

$1^1/_2$ tsp chopped fresh sage

1 garlic clove, coarsely chopped

$2/_3$ cup heavy cream

salt and pepper

fresh bay leaves or sage leaves, to garnish

Melba toast, to serve

Melt 3 tablespoons of the butter in a large, heavy-bottom skillet. Add the chicken livers and cook over medium heat for about 4 minutes on each side. They should be browned on the outside but still pink in the middle. Transfer to a food processor and process until finely chopped.

Stir the Marsala or brandy into the skillet, scraping up any sediment with a wooden spoon, then add to the food processor with the sage, garlic, and $3^1/_2$ oz/100 g of the remaining butter. Process until smooth. Add the cream, season with salt and pepper, and process until thoroughly combined and smooth. Spoon the pâté into a dish or individual ramekins, level the surface, and let cool completely.

Melt the remaining butter, then spoon it over the surface of the pâté. Decorate with herb leaves, cool, then let chill in the refrigerator. Serve with Melba toast.

Cranberry sauce

 extremely easy   10 minutes   10–12 minutes   serves 8

INGREDIENTS

thinly pared rind and juice
of 1 lemon

thinly pared rind and juice
of 1 orange

3 cups cranberries, thawed if
frozen

scant ³/₄ cup superfine sugar

2 tbsp arrowroot mixed with
3 tbsp cold water

Cut strips of lemon and orange rind into thin shreds and place in a heavy-bottom pan. If using fresh cranberries, rinse well and remove any stalks. Add the berries, citrus juice, and sugar and cook over medium heat, stirring occasionally, for about 5 minutes, until the berries start to burst.

Strain the juice into a clean pan and set aside the cranberries. Stir the arrowroot mixture into the juice, then bring to a boil, stirring constantly, until the sauce is smooth and thickened. Remove from the heat and stir in the reserved cranberries.

Transfer the cranberry sauce to a bowl and let cool, then cover with plastic wrap and let chill in the refrigerator.

Poached salmon

 easy   20 minutes, plus cooling    30 minutes   serves 8–12

INGREDIENTS

17 cups water
6 tbsp white wine vinegar
1 large onion, sliced
2 carrots, sliced
1¹/₂ tbsp salt
1 tsp black peppercorns
1 x 6-lb/2.7-kg salmon, cleaned, with gills and eyes removed

TO SERVE
mixed salad greens
1 cucumber, thinly sliced
1 pimiento-stuffed olive
lemon wedges
Mayonnaise (see page 90), already prepared

To make the stock (court-bouillon) in which to poach the fish, put the water, vinegar, onion, carrots, salt, and peppercorns in a large fish poacher, or covered roasting pan, and bring to a boil. Lower the heat and let simmer for 20 minutes. Remove the tray (if using the poacher) and lay the salmon on it. Lower it into the court-bouillon, cover, bring back to simmering point, and cook for 5 minutes. Turn off the heat and leave the fish, covered, to cool in the liquid.

When the fish is cold, lift it out of the poacher on the tray, and drain well. Using 2 spatulas, carefully transfer to a board. Using a sharp knife, slit the skin along the backbone and around the back of the head, then peel off. Carefully turn the fish over and peel off the skin on the other side.

To serve, line a serving platter with mixed salad greens, and carefully transfer the salmon to the platter. Arrange the cucumber slices decoratively over part or all of the fish. Halve the olive and place a half in the exposed eye socket. Garnish with lemon wedges and serve with a bowl of mayonnaise.

Apple pies

INGREDIENTS

2 1/2 cups all-purpose flour, plus extra for dusting

6 oz/175 g butter, at room temperature

scant 1/2 cup superfine sugar, plus extra for sprinkling

2 egg yolks

1–2 drops vanilla extract

2 lb/900 g cooking apples, peeled, cored, and thinly sliced

2 tbsp lemon juice

1/2 tsp ground allspice

1/2 tsp ground cinnamon

1/4 tsp ground ginger

1/4 tsp freshly grated nutmeg

Sift all but 2 tablespoons of the flour onto a counter or board and make a well in the center. Place the butter, sugar, egg yolks, and vanilla extract in the well and mix together with your fingertips. Very gradually work in the flour with your fingertips until it is fully incorporated. If the dough seems too crumbly, add a small amount of ice water. Shape into a ball, wrap in plastic wrap, and let chill for 30 minutes.

Place the apples, reserved flour, lemon juice, allspice, cinnamon, ginger, and nutmeg in a bowl and toss well. Preheat the oven to 375°F/190°C. Divide the dough in half. Roll out one piece on a lightly floured counter and stamp out 18–20 circles with a 3-inch/7.5-cm fluted cutter. Use these to line deep tartlet pans. Divide the apple mixture between them. Do not overfill; they should be about two-thirds full. Roll out the second piece of dough and stamp out 18–20 circles with a 2 1/2-inch/6-cm fluted cutter. Cover the pies with the smaller dough circles, sealing the edges well. Make 2 small slits in each lid. If you like, roll out the dough trimmings, cut out small holly leaves, brush with water, and use to decorate the tops of the pies. Bake for 20 minutes, until golden brown.

Using a spatula, transfer the pies to a wire rack, and sprinkle with superfine sugar. Serve warm or at room temperature.

Orange rum hard sauce

 extremely easy 10 minutes, plus chilling none serves 6–8

INGREDIENTS

4 oz/115 g unsalted butter, at room temperature
generous 1/2 cup (packed) brown sugar
finely grated rind of 1 orange
pinch of allspice
3 tbsp rum

Cream the butter in a bowl until it is very smooth and soft. Gradually beat in the sugar, orange rind, and allspice. Add the rum, a little at a time, beating well after each addition and taking care not to let the mixture curdle.

Spoon the orange rum hard sauce into a small serving dish, cover with plastic wrap, and let chill until required.

$\mathcal{H}$ard sauce

 extremely easy   15 minutes, plus chilling   none   serves 6–8

INGREDIENTS

4 oz/115 g unsalted butter,
  at room temperature
generous ¹/₄ cup superfine sugar
¹/₂ cup confectioners' sugar,
  sifted
3 tbsp brandy

Cream the butter in a bowl until it is very smooth and soft. Gradually beat in both types of sugar. Add the brandy, a little at a time, beating well after each addition and taking care not to let the mixture curdle.

Spread out the butter on a sheet of foil and let chill until firm. Stamp out decorative shapes with tiny cutters and place on a baking sheet or flat tray. Cover and let chill until required.

$\mathcal{H}$ot rum punch

 extremely easy   15 minutes   none   makes 18 cups

INGREDIENTS

3¹/₂ cups rum
3¹/₂ cups brandy
2¹/₂ cups freshly squeezed lemon juice
3–4 tbsp superfine sugar
scant 8¹/₂ cups boiling water
orange and lemon slices, to decorate

Mix together the rum, brandy, lemon juice, and 3 tablespoons of the sugar in a punch bowl or large mixing bowl. Pour in the boiling water and stir well to mix. Taste and add more sugar if required. Decorate with the fruit slices and serve at once in heatproof glasses.

Mulled ale and Mulled wine

MULLED ALE INGREDIENTS

generous 10¹/₂ cups strong ale
1¹/₄ cups brandy
2 tbsp superfine sugar
large pinch of ground cloves
large pinch of ground ginger

MULLED WINE INGREDIENTS

5 oranges
50 cloves
thinly pared rind and juice of
 4 lemons
3¹/₂ cups water
generous ¹/₂ cup superfine sugar
2 cinnamon sticks
scant 8¹/₂ cups red wine
²/₃ cup brandy

Mulled ale

 extremely easy   5 minutes   5–8 minutes   makes 12 cups

Put all the ingredients in a heavy-bottom pan and heat gently, stirring until the sugar has dissolved. Continue to heat so that it is simmering but not boiling. Remove the pan from the heat and serve the ale at once in heatproof glasses.

Mulled wine

 extremely easy   15 minutes, plus 10 minutes standing   10–15 minutes   makes about 15 cups

Prick the skins of 3 of the oranges all over with a fork and stud with the cloves, then set aside. Thinly pare the rind and squeeze the juice from the remaining oranges.

Put the orange rind and juice, lemon rind and juice, water, sugar, and cinnamon in a heavy-bottom pan and bring to a boil over medium heat, stirring occasionally until the sugar has dissolved. Boil for 2 minutes without stirring, then remove from the heat, stir once and let stand for 10 minutes. Strain the liquid into a heatproof pitcher, pressing down on the contents of the strainer to extract all the juice.

Pour the wine into another pan and add the strained spiced juices, the brandy, and clove-studded oranges. Let simmer gently without boiling, then remove the pan from the heat. Strain into heatproof glasses and serve the wine at once.

Stuffed dates

 extremely easy 20 minutes none 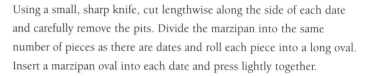 serves 6–8

INGREDIENTS

1 lb 2 oz/500 g fresh dates
9¹/₂ oz/275 g marzipan

Using a small, sharp knife, cut lengthwise along the side of each date and carefully remove the pits. Divide the marzipan into the same number of pieces as there are dates and roll each piece into a long oval. Insert a marzipan oval into each date and press lightly together.

Place the stuffed dates in petit four or candy cases and store in an airtight container in the refrigerator until about 30 minutes before they are required. Bring to room temperature before serving.

CHRISTMAS DAY: THE HIGHLIGHT OF THE CELEBRATIONS

Christmas dinner is hard work, but it's worth it as it is the focal point of the family celebrations. The recipes in this chapter provide fail-safe guidance for cooking all the traditional favorites, from Roast Turkey (see page 62) to Brussels Sprouts with Chestnuts (see page 73).

Start the day on a festive note with Scrambled Eggs with Smoked Salmon (see page 54) and, if you really want to push the boat out, serve them with Buck's Fizz, one of the Champagne Cocktails (see page 56). However, you might prefer to delay the cocktails until the roast is safely in the oven and your guests have arrived.

There is a wide choice of special dishes for Christmas Day, including a Vegetarian Roast (see page 69) and two different kinds of dressing (see pages 59 and 60), both of which are suitable for turkey and goose. The Festive Shrimp Cocktail (see page 76) makes a tempting appetizer that can be prepared quickly and easily in the morning. Don't forget to steam the Plum pudding on Christmas morning.

Finally, when the feasting is over and before you even contemplate cleaning up in the kitchen, treat yourself and your guests to a glass of Irish Coffee (see page 78).

Scrambled eggs with smoked salmon

 very easy   10 minutes   5 minutes   serves 4

INGREDIENTS

4 oz/115 g smoked salmon slices
6 large eggs
3 tbsp light cream
3 tbsp butter
salt and pepper
2 slices of toast, buttered and
   cut into 8 triangles, to serve

Using a sharp knife, chop the smoked salmon. Lightly beat the eggs with the cream until just combined.

Melt the butter in a heavy-bottom pan over low heat. When it starts to foam, pour in the egg mixture, and cook, stirring constantly, until creamy and just starting to set. Turn off the heat and stir in the smoked salmon. Remove the pan from the stove and season the scrambled eggs with salt and pepper to taste, remembering that the fish will be quite salty.

Divide the scrambled egg mixture between warm plates and serve at once with the toast triangles.

*C*hampagne cocktails

 extremely easy  2 minutes each none each recipe serves 1

INGREDIENTS

BUCK'S FIZZ
2 tbsp chilled fresh orange juice
dash of grenadine
chilled champagne

BLUE CHAMPAGNE
1 tsp blue curaçao
chilled champagne

CARIBBEAN CHRISTMAS CHAMPAGNE
1/2 tsp crème de banane
1/2 tsp white rum
chilled champagne

For the buck's fizz, pour the orange juice into a chilled champagne flute, add a dash of grenadine, and stir well. Top off with chilled champagne and serve at once.

For the blue champagne, pour the curaçao into a chilled champagne flute and swirl to coat the sides of the glass. Fill with chilled champagne and serve at once.

For the Caribbean Christmas champagne, pour the crème de banane and rum into a chilled champagne flute. Fill with chilled champagne and stir gently. Serve at once.

Chestnut and sausage dressing

 extremely easy   15 minutes   30–40 minutes   serves 6–8

INGREDIENTS

8 oz/225 g pork sausagemeat

generous 1 cup unsweetened chestnut purée

scant ⁵/₈ cup walnuts, chopped

²/₃ cup no-soak dried apricots, chopped

2 tbsp chopped fresh parsley

2 tbsp chopped fresh chives

2 tsp chopped fresh sage

4–5 tbsp heavy cream

salt and pepper

Combine the sausagemeat and chestnut purée in a bowl, then stir in the walnuts, apricots, parsley, chives, and sage. Stir in enough heavy cream to make a firm, but not dry, mixture. Season with salt and pepper.

If you are planning to stuff a turkey or goose, fill only the neck cavity. It is safer and more reliable to cook the dressing separately, either rolled into small balls and placed on a baking sheet or spooned into an ovenproof dish.

Cook the separate dressing in an oven for 30–40 minutes at 375°F/190°C. It should be allowed a longer time if you are roasting a bird at a lower temperature in the same oven.

Mushroom dressing

  extremely easy 10 minutes 40–50 minutes  serves 6–8

INGREDIENTS

2 oz/55 g butter
3 shallots, chopped
8 oz/225 g mixed wild and
  cultivated mushrooms, chopped
4 oz/115 g pork sausagemeat
1¹/₂ cups fresh white
  bread crumbs
few drops of truffle oil (optional)
salt and pepper

Melt the butter in a heavy-bottom skillet over low heat. Add the shallots and cook, stirring occasionally, for about 5 minutes, until softened. Add the mushrooms and cook, stirring occasionally, until their juices have evaporated. Transfer the mixture to a bowl and stir in the sausagemeat, bread crumbs, and truffle oil, if you like, and season to taste with salt and pepper.

If you are planning to stuff a turkey or goose, fill only the neck cavity. It is safer and more reliable to cook the dressing separately, either rolled into small balls and placed on a baking sheet or spooned into an ovenproof dish.

Cook the separate dressing in an oven for 30–40 minutes at 375°F/190°C. It should be allowed a longer time if you are roasting a bird at a lower temperature in the same oven.

Roast turkey with bread sauce

 very easy   20 minutes   3½ hours   serves 8

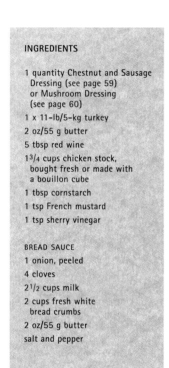

INGREDIENTS

1 quantity Chestnut and Sausage
  Dressing (see page 59)
  or Mushroom Dressing
  (see page 60)

1 x 11-lb/5-kg turkey

2 oz/55 g butter

5 tbsp red wine

1¾ cups chicken stock,
  bought fresh or made with
  a bouillon cube

1 tbsp cornstarch

1 tsp French mustard

1 tsp sherry vinegar

BREAD SAUCE

1 onion, peeled

4 cloves

2½ cups milk

2 cups fresh white
  bread crumbs

2 oz/55 g butter

salt and pepper

Preheat the oven to 425°F/220°C. Spoon the dressing into the neck cavity of the turkey and close the flap of skin with a skewer. Place the bird in a large roasting pan and rub all over with 3 tablespoons of the butter. Roast for 1 hour, then lower the oven temperature to 350°F/180°C and roast for an additional 2½ hours. You may need to pour off the fat from the roasting pan occasionally.

Meanwhile, make the bread sauce. Stud the onion with the cloves, then place in a pan with the milk, bread crumbs, and butter. Bring just to boiling point over low heat, then remove from the heat and let stand in a warm place to infuse. Just before serving, remove the onion and reheat the sauce gently, beating well with a wooden spoon. Season to taste with salt and pepper.

Check that the turkey is cooked by inserting a skewer or the point of a sharp knife into the thigh; if the juices run clear, it is ready. Transfer the bird to a carving board, cover loosely with foil, and let rest.

To make the gravy, skim off the fat from the roasting pan then place the pan over medium heat. Add the red wine and stir with a wooden spoon, scraping up the sediment from the bottom of the pan. Stir in the chicken stock. Mix the cornstarch, mustard, vinegar, and 2 teaspoons water together in a small bowl, then stir into the wine and stock. Bring to a boil, stirring constantly until thickened and smooth. Stir in the remaining butter.

Carve the turkey and serve with the warm bread sauce and all the trimmings—including dressing, potatoes, and gravy.

Roast goose

 very easy   15 minutes   3–3¼ hours   serves 8

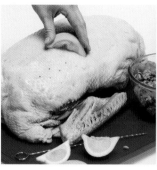 

INGREDIENTS

1 x 9-lb/4-kg goose

1 lemon, cut into quarters

1 quantity Chestnut and Sausage
Dressing (see page 59)
or Mushroom Dressing
(see page 60)

5 tbsp medium sherry

1¾ cups chicken stock
bought fresh or made with
a bouillon cube

1 tbsp cornstarch

1 tsp Dijon mustard

1 tsp red wine vinegar

1 tbsp butter

salt and pepper

Preheat the oven to 450°F/230°C. Prick the skin of the goose all over with a fine skewer or fork. Rub with 3 of the lemon quarters and season with salt and pepper. Squeeze the juice from the remaining lemon quarter into the cavity. Spoon the dressing into the neck cavity of the bird and fasten the flap of skin with a skewer.

Place the goose, breast-side down, on a wire rack set over a roasting pan and roast for 15 minutes. Lower the oven temperature to 350°F/180°C and roast for an additional 2¾–3 hours. Halfway through the cooking time, turn the goose onto its back. You may need to pour off the fat from the roasting pan occasionally. Save it for making perfect roast potatoes today or on another day (see page 70).

Check that the goose is cooked by inserting a skewer or the point of a sharp knife into the thigh; if the juices run clear, it is ready. Transfer the bird to a carving board, cover loosely with foil, and let rest.

To make the gravy, skim off the fat from the roasting pan then place the pan over medium heat. Add the sherry and stir with a wooden spoon, scraping up the sediment from the bottom of the pan. Stir in the chicken stock. Mix together the cornstarch, mustard, vinegar, and 2 teaspoons water in a small bowl, then stir into the wine and stock. Bring to a boil, stirring constantly until thickened and smooth. Whisk in the butter.

Carve the goose and serve with all the trimmings—including the dressing, potatoes, and gravy.

Glazed ham

INGREDIENTS

1 x 9-lb/4-kg ham joint
1 apple, cored and chopped
1 onion, chopped
1¹/₄ cups hard cider
6 black peppercorns
1 bouquet garni
bay leaf
about 50 cloves
4 tbsp raw brown sugar

Put the ham in a large pan and add enough cold water to cover. Bring to a boil and skim off the scum that rises to the surface. Lower the heat and let simmer for 30 minutes. Drain the ham and return to the pan. Add the apple, onion, cider, peppercorns, bouquet garni, bay leaf, and a few of the cloves. Pour in enough fresh water to cover and return to a boil. Cover and let simmer for 3 hours 20 minutes.

Preheat the oven to 400°F/200°C. Take the pan off the heat and set aside to cool slightly. Remove the ham from the cooking liquid and, while it is still warm, loosen the rind with a sharp knife, then peel it off and discard. Score the fat into diamond shapes and stud with the remaining cloves. Place the ham on a rack in a roasting pan and sprinkle with the sugar. Roast, basting occasionally with the cooking liquid, for 20 minutes. Serve hot with all the trimmings, or cold later.

*V*egetarian roast

 very easy   30 minutes, plus cooling and standing   1 hour 30 minutes   serves 8

INGREDIENTS

1 cup walnuts
generous 3/4 cup hazelnuts
2 oz/55 g butter or vegetarian margarine
2 onions, finely chopped
1 large carrot, finely chopped
4 oz/115 g mushrooms, finely chopped
2 celery stalks, finely chopped
dash of Tabasco sauce
oil, for oiling
generous 1/2 cup red lentils, soaked in water for 30 minutes and drained
2 tbsp Worcestershire sauce
2 tbsp tomato ketchup
1 egg, lightly beaten
3 tbsp chopped fresh parsley
salt
Cranberry Sauce (see page 36), to serve

Place the nuts in a food processor and grind until fairly fine, then set aside. Melt the butter or margarine in a large pan and add the onions, carrot, mushrooms, and celery. Cook over medium heat, stirring occasionally, for 5 minutes. Stir in the Tabasco and cook for a few seconds more. Remove the pan from the heat and let cool.

Preheat the oven to 375°F/190°C. Oil and line a 2-lb/1-kg loaf pan with foil or waxed paper. Transfer the vegetable mixture to a large bowl and stir in the ground nuts, lentils, Worcestershire sauce, tomato ketchup, egg, and parsley. Season with salt.

Spoon the mixture into the prepared pan, pressing it in firmly, and roast for 1¼ hours, until just firm to the touch. After 45 minutes, cover the surface with lightly oiled waxed paper.

Remove the pan from the oven and let stand for 15 minutes. Peel off the paper, turn out, and cut into slices. Serve hot or cold with cranberry sauce.

Perfect roast potatoes

 extremely easy 10 minutes 1 hr 25 minutes serves 8

INGREDIENTS

2¹/₂ oz/70 g goose fat or duck fat or 5 tbsp olive oil

coarse sea salt

2 lb 4 oz/1 kg even-size potatoes, peeled

8 fresh rosemary sprigs, to garnish

Preheat the oven to 450°F/230°C. Put the fat or oil in a large roasting pan, sprinkle generously with sea salt, and place in the oven.

Meanwhile, cook the potatoes in a large pan of boiling water for 8–10 minutes, until parboiled. Drain well, and if the potatoes are large, cut them in half. Return the potatoes to the pan and shake vigorously to coarsen their outsides.

Arrange the potatoes in a single layer in the hot pan and roast for 45 minutes. If they look as if they are starting to char around the edges, lower the oven temperature to 400°F/200°C. Turn the potatoes over and roast for an additional 30 minutes, until crisp. Serve garnished with sprigs of rosemary.

Brussels sprouts with chestnuts

 very easy 20 minutes  55 minutes serves 8

INGREDIENTS

1 lb/450 g fresh chestnuts
1 cup milk
2 oz/55 g butter
1/2 small onion, finely chopped
1 lb 9 oz/700 g Brussels sprouts,
  trimmed with a small cross in
  the base

First cook the chestnuts. Bring a pan of water to a boil, add the chestnuts, return to a boil, and cook for 8–10 minutes. Drain and, when cool enough to handle, peel them.

Place the peeled chestnuts in a pan and add the milk and enough water to cover. Bring to a boil, lower the heat, and let simmer for 15 minutes. Drain and set aside.

Melt the butter in a heavy-bottom sauté pan. Add the onion and cook over low heat, stirring occasionally, for 5 minutes, until softened. Add the Brussels sprouts and 3 tablespoons water. Cover and cook for 8 minutes. Stir in the chestnuts, re-cover the pan and cook for an additional 5 minutes or until the Brussels sprouts are tender. Transfer to a warm serving dish and serve at once.

Glazed parsnips

  extremely easy 10 minutes 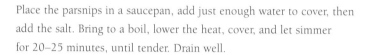 35–45 minutes serves 8

Place the parsnips in a saucepan, add just enough water to cover, then add the salt. Bring to a boil, lower the heat, cover, and let simmer for 20–25 minutes, until tender. Drain well.

Melt the butter in a heavy-bottom sauté pan or preheated wok. Add the parsnips and toss well. Sprinkle with the sugar then cook, stirring frequently, to prevent the sugar from sticking to the pan or burning. Cook the parsnips for 10–15 minutes, until golden and glazed. Transfer to a warm serving dish and serve immediately.

Festive shrimp cocktail

  extremely easy   30 minutes   none   serves 8

INGREDIENTS

1¹/₂ cups Mayonnaise
  (see page 90), already prepared
¹/₂ cup tomato ketchup
1 tsp chili sauce
1 tsp Worcestershire sauce
2 lb 4 oz/1 kg cooked jumbo
  shrimp
2 ruby grapefruits
lettuce leaves, shredded
2 avocados, peeled, pitted,
  and diced

TO GARNISH
lime slices
dill sprigs

Mix together the mayonnaise, tomato ketchup, chili sauce, and Worcestershire sauce in a small bowl. Cover with plastic wrap and place in the refrigerator until required.

Remove the heads from the shrimp and peel off the shells, leaving the tails intact. Slit along the length of the back of each shrimp with a sharp knife and remove the dark vein. Cut off a slice from the top and bottom of each grapefruit, then peel off the skin and all the white pith. Cut between the membranes to separate the segments.

When ready to serve, make a bed of shredded lettuce in the base of 8 glass dishes. Divide the shrimp, grapefruit segments, and avocados between them and spoon over the mayonnaise dressing. Serve garnished with lime slices and dill sprigs.

Irish coffee

 very easy   10 minutes   5 minutes   serves 8

INGREDIENTS

8 sugar lumps
1/2 cup water
1 cup Irish whiskey
2 1/2 cups freshly made strong
   black coffee
1 cup heavy cream, chilled

Place the sugar lumps and water in a pan and heat gently, stirring until the sugar has dissolved. Divide between 8 heatproof glasses. Add about 2 tablespoons whiskey to each glass, then pour in the coffee. Stir well.

Hold a teaspoon against the side of a glass with the back of the spoon facing upward. Pour about 2 tablespoons of cream over the spoon so that it floats on top of the coffee. Repeat with the remaining glasses, then serve.

THE DAY AFTER CHRISTMAS: LUXURY LEFTOVERS

After the hectic effort of preparing the Christmas meal the day before and the heroic cleaning up afterward, no one wants to spend much time in the kitchen the following day. Nevertheless, simply serving slices of cold turkey and ham can be something of an anticlimax. The recipes in this chapter suggest more interesting ways of serving leftovers that don't involve too much cooking and are perfect for the more informal but still festive atmosphere. You may be surprised how easily appetites can be tempted even after a sumptuous Christmas dinner, a late night, and lots of excitement.

Succulent Turkey Chasseur (see page 82), Crisp Turkey Pie (see page 84), and Turkey Curry (see page 87) are impressive dishes that are sure to be popular. Eggs Benedict (see page 88) provides the perfect opportunity to use up any leftover ham and is ideal for a casual brunch. If you are planning to serve simple cold meats, why not brighten them up with a colorful Waldorf Salad or a crunchy home-made Coleslaw (see page 90) along with salad greens.

Finally, if you're still in the mood for self-indulgence but don't fancy cold Plum Pudding, round off your day after Christmas feast with a rich, creamy Tipsy Cake (see page 93) or a deliciously refreshing Fruit Compote (see page 94).

Turkey chasseur

 easy   20 minutes   35–40 minutes   serves 6

INGREDIENTS

2 tbsp butter
1 onion, chopped
4 oz/115 g mushrooms, sliced
6 tbsp white wine
1 tbsp tomato paste
1 lb 10 oz/750 g cooked
  turkey, cubed
2 tbsp chopped fresh parsley,
  to garnish

SAUCE
2 oz/55 g butter
1 bacon slice, chopped
1 onion, chopped
2 oz/55 g mushrooms, sliced
2 tomatoes, peeled and chopped
scant $^1/_4$ cup all-purpose flour
$1^1/_4$ cups beef stock, bought
  fresh or made with
  a bouillon cube
bouquet garni
salt and pepper
2 tbsp medium sherry

First, make the sauce. Melt the butter in a heavy-bottom pan. Add the bacon, onion, mushrooms, and tomatoes and cook over low heat, stirring occasionally, for 5 minutes. Stir in the flour and cook, stirring constantly, until it starts to turn golden. Gradually stir in the stock and bring to a boil. Continue to stir until thickened and smooth. Add the bouquet garni and season with salt and pepper. Lower the heat and let simmer for 15 minutes. Let cool slightly, then transfer to a blender or food processor and process until smooth. Stir in the sherry.

Melt the butter in a pan and add the onion and mushrooms. Cook over low heat, stirring occasionally, for 5 minutes. Stir in the prepared sauce, wine, and tomato paste and simmer for an additional 5 minutes. Add the cubed turkey and heat through gently. Transfer to a warm serving dish, garnish with the parsley, and serve at once.

Turkey pie

INGREDIENTS

2 oz/55 g butter
2 tbsp all-purpose flour
1 cup chicken stock, bought
  fresh or made with
  a bouillon cube
3 tbsp heavy cream
salt and pepper
1 onion, chopped
2 carrots, sliced
2 celery stalks, chopped
2 oz/55 g mushrooms, sliced
1 lb/450 g cooked turkey, diced
$^1/_2$ cup frozen peas
1 egg, lightly beaten

PIE DOUGH

scant 1$^5/_8$ cups all-purpose flour,
  plus extra for dusting
pinch of salt
4 oz/115 g margarine
2 oz/55 g lard or
  vegetable shortening
1–2 tbsp iced water

First, make the pie dough. Sift the flour and a pinch of salt into a bowl. Add the margarine and lard or vegetable shortening and cut them into the flour, then rub in with your fingertips until the mixture resembles bread crumbs. Mix in enough iced water to make a firm dough. Gather the dough into a ball, wrap in plastic wrap, and let chill in the refrigerator for 30 minutes.

Preheat the oven to 375°F/190°C. Melt half the butter in a pan, stir in the flour, and cook, stirring constantly, for 1 minute. Gradually whisk in the stock and bring to a boil, whisking constantly. Let simmer for 2 minutes, then stir in the cream. Season with salt and pepper and set aside.

Melt the remaining butter in a large skillet. Add the onion and carrots and cook over low heat, stirring occasionally, for 5 minutes. Add the celery and mushrooms and cook for an additional 5 minutes, then stir in the turkey and peas. Stir the turkey mixture into the cream sauce, then transfer to a large pie dish.

Roll out the dough on a lightly floured counter to about $^1/_8$ inch/3 mm thick. Cut out a rectangle about 1 inch/2.5 cm larger than the dish and lay it over the filling. Crimp the edges, cut 3–4 slits in the top to allow steam to escape and brush with the beaten egg. Roll out the trimmings and cut out shapes to decorate the pie if you like. Bake the pie for 30 minutes, until golden brown. Serve at once.

Turkey curry

extremely easy   10 minutes, plus cooling   15 minutes   serves 6

INGREDIENTS

1 tbsp butter
2 shallots, chopped
1 tbsp tomato paste
1 tbsp curry paste
1/2 cup red wine
2 tbsp lemon juice
12 tbsp apricot jelly
1 1/4 cups Mayonnaise (see page 90)
1/2 cup heavy cream
salt and pepper
1 lb 10 oz/750 g cold cooked turkey, diced
green salad, to serve

Melt the butter in a small skillet. Add the shallots and cook over low heat, stirring occasionally, for 5 minutes, until softened. Add the tomato paste, curry paste, wine, and lemon juice and let simmer gently for an additional 10 minutes. Stir in the apricot jelly, push through a strainer, and set aside to cool.

Beat the cooled mixture into the mayonnaise. Whip the cream and fold it into the mayonnaise. Season to taste with salt and pepper and stir in the diced turkey. Serve with a green salad.

$\mathcal{E}$ggs benedict

 very easy   10 minutes   25 minutes   serves 6

INGREDIENTS

6 eggs
3 English muffins
3 slices cooked ham

HOLLANDAISE SAUCE
3 egg yolks
1 tbsp lemon juice
salt and cayenne pepper
8 oz/225 g unsalted butter, diced
ground pepper, for dusting

First, make the hollandaise sauce. Whisk together the egg yolks, lemon juice, and salt and cayenne pepper in a heatproof bowl over a pan of barely simmering water. Add the diced butter, whisking constantly until the butter has melted. Remove from the heat and continue whisking until the sauce is thick and creamy. Keep warm over the hot water.

Meanwhile, preheat the broiler. Split the English muffins in half. Using a sharp knife, cut out circles from the ham the same size as the English muffin halves. Place the ham circles under the broiler and cook until hot and golden.

Bring a pan of water to a boil, then lower the heat so that the water is barely simmering and poach the eggs, for 3–4 minutes, until the whites are just firm. Drain with a slotted spoon and trim the whites, if necessary.

Meanwhile, toast the English muffin halves. Place on 6 warmed plates, top with a slice of ham and an egg, and spoon over the sauce. Add the pepper and serve at once.

Coleslaw and Waldorf salad

Coleslaw

 extremely easy   15 minutes   none   serves 6

COLESLAW INGREDIENTS

1/2 white cabbage
2 carrots, grated
1 eating apple, cored and chopped
4 scallions, chopped
1 red bell pepper, seeded and chopped
2 celery stalks, chopped

MAYONNAISE
2 egg yolks
4 tsp lemon juice
1 tsp mustard powder
scant 1 1/4 cups corn oil
1–2 tbsp hot water

WALDORF SALAD INGREDIENTS

3 eating apples, cored and chopped
3 celery stalks, chopped
3/4 cup walnut halves
1 tbsp lemon juice
1/2 cup Mayonnaise (see above)
lettuce leaves, to serve

First make the mayonnaise. Put the egg yolks, half the lemon juice, and the mustard powder in a blender or food processor and process until combined. With the motor running, gradually add the oil in a thin stream through the feeder tube, processing until it is fully incorporated. Scrape the mayonnaise into a bowl and add enough hot water to give the required consistency.

Using a sharp knife, remove the core from the cabbage and shred the leaves finely. Mix the cabbage, carrots, apple, scallions, red bell pepper, and celery in a serving bowl.

Stir the remaining lemon juice into the mayonnaise, then stir into the salad. Mix well and serve at once.

Waldorf salad

 extremely easy   10 minutes   none   serves 6

Mix together the apples, celery, and walnut halves in a bowl and sprinkle with the lemon juice. Add the mayonnaise and stir gently to mix.

Line a serving dish with lettuce leaves and spoon the salad over. Serve at room temperature.

Tipsy cake

 easy   15 minutes, plus infusing and chilling    10 minutes   serves 6

INGREDIENTS

1 x 9-inch/23-cm sponge cake
4 tbsp raspberry jelly
²/₃ cup medium sherry
1 cup heavy cream
¹/₃ cup candied cherries
1 oz/25 g angelica, cut into fine strips
¹/₂ cup slivered almonds

VANILLA CREAM
2 cups milk
1 vanilla bean
4 egg yolks
generous ¹/₄ cup superfine sugar

First, make the vanilla cream. Place the milk and vanilla bean in a heatproof bowl set over a pan of simmering water and bring to just below boiling point. Remove the bowl from the heat, cover, and set aside to infuse for 10 minutes. Remove the vanilla bean, wipe dry, and set aside for use in another recipe. Beat the egg yolks with the sugar in another bowl until smooth and creamy, then gradually whisk in the milk. Return the mixture to the heatproof bowl and set over simmering water. Heat gently, stirring constantly, for about 5 minutes, until thickened. Remove from the heat.

Slice the cake in half horizontally, spread one half with the jelly, and lay the other half on top. Pour the sherry over the cake, followed by the hot vanilla cream. Let cool, then let chill in the refrigerator.

Beat the cream until soft peaks form, then spread it over the top and sides of the cake with a spatula to cover the vanilla cream completely. Decorate with the cherries, angelica, and almonds and keep in the refrigerator until required.

Fruit compote

 extremely easy

 10 minutes, plus chilling

 20 minutes

 serves 6

INGREDIENTS

1¹/2 cups raspberries
1¹/2 cups black currants
scant ¹/2 cup superfine sugar
²/3 cup water
2 tbsp arrowroot mixed with a little cold water
2 tbsp crème de cassis
heavy cream, to serve

Put the raspberries, black currants, sugar, and water into a heavy-bottom pan, cover, and cook over low heat for 15 minutes, until the fruit is soft.

Stir the arrowroot paste and place in a pan. Bring the mixture to a boil, stirring constantly until thickened. Remove from the heat and let cool slightly, before stirring in the black currants, raspberries, and the crème de cassis.

Pour the compote into a glass bowl, let cool, then let chill for at least 1 hour. To serve, divide the compote between 6 decorative glass dishes, and top with a swirl of cream.

Index